Little Secrets of Happiness

*They'll dazzle your heart
each day of the month*

J. Donald Walters

Hardbound edition, first printing 1994

ISBN 1-56589-604-1

10 9 8 7 6 5 4 3 2

PRINTED IN HONG KONG

Crystal ❦ *Clarity*
P U B L I S H E R S

14618 Tyler Foote Road, Nevada City, CA 95959
1 (800) 424-1055

Keep one page open
    each day.
Think of the secret on that page.
Feel what it says.
Hold it inside your heart so deeply
    you'll find golden dreams awaiting you
        in sleep.
Every morning,
    when you awake,
    a new, secret friend
    will be there,
        smiling within you.

Day 1

Your happiness grows when you help other people. But the less you try to help them, the more it shrivels and dries up. For happiness is like a plant: It must be watered daily with giving thoughts and actions.

The secret of happiness is smiling at others; comforting them when they're sad. For just as a candle shines more brightly in a room if the walls are white, so our happiness shines more brightly when reflected back to us in the smiles of others.

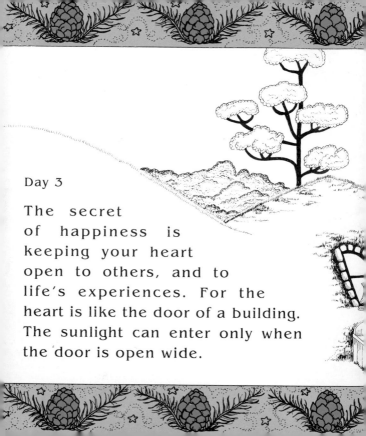

Day 3

The secret
of happiness is
keeping your heart
open to others, and to
life's experiences. For the
heart is like the door of a building.
The sunlight can enter only when
the door is open wide.

Day 4

Happiness comes from putting out energy; from doing things yourself, and not from just sitting there, watching TV.

Happiness comes from accepting others as they are, instead of wishing they were somehow otherwise. How boring life would be if everyone were alike! Would a garden be any fun, if all its flowers were purple?

Day 5

Day 6

Happiness means making others happy. A flowery meadow needs surroundings of trees, not of ugly buildings. Surround your life's meadow with happiness.

Day 7

The secret of happiness is understanding that friendship is more precious than things; more precious than getting your own way; more precious than being right in matters where principles are not at stake.

Day 8

Happiness means accepting whatever comes, and telling yourself always, "I am free, inside!"

Day 9

Happiness comes to those who give love freely, and who don't demand that others love them first. Be generous like the sun's rays, which shine without asking first whether people deserve their warmth.

Day 10

The secret of happiness is not wishing harm to anyone. Be kind, if you want to receive kindness back from life.

Day 11

The secret of happiness is simply this: BE happy! Don't wait for others or for anything to make you happy. Happiness is like an underground stream: To find it, one must dig for it. Look for it deep inside yourself.

Day 12

The secret of happiness is learning how to pass through life's storms with a peaceful heart, its aura enclosing you in a cloak of light.

Happiness is NOW! It isn't tomorrow. It isn't yesterday. Happiness is like a morning glory: Yesterday's won't bloom again; tomorrow's hasn't opened yet. Only today's flower can be enjoyed today. Be happy this very moment, and you'll learn how to be happy always.

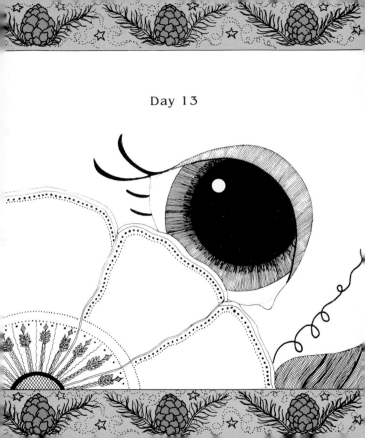

Day 13

Day 14

Happiness comes from being contented with less. Imaginary needs are like openings in a dam: They empty the mind's lake of its waters of happiness.

Day 15

Happiness is seeing God's blessings in everything—even in pain. For painful experiences can make one stronger. There would be no peaches, if it weren't also for the rain.

Day 16

One important secret of happiness is standing by your parents, your brothers and sisters, your friends and relatives. As you are true to them, so be true to everyone. See your faithfulness to them as a balloon of light, expanding to include all people, all creatures as your own.

The secret of happiness is not to be stu
you act important. But if you give *the*
you go. Do you like feeling big? Then remi
off the biggest smell.

Day 17

p. People will only turn away from you if
mportance, you'll have friends everywhere
ourself, it's the biggest skunk that gives

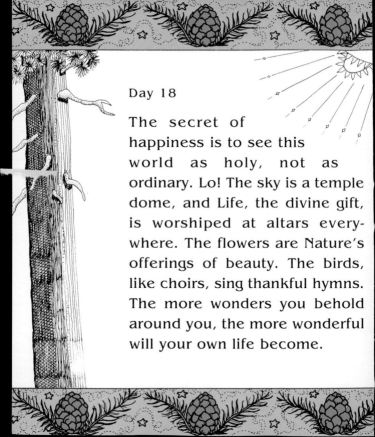

Day 18

The secret of happiness is to see this world as holy, not as ordinary. Lo! The sky is a temple dome, and Life, the divine gift, is worshiped at altars everywhere. The flowers are Nature's offerings of beauty. The birds, like choirs, sing thankful hymns. The more wonders you behold around you, the more wonderful will your own life become.

Day 19

The secret of happiness is laughing *with* others, as their friend, and not *at* them, as their judge.

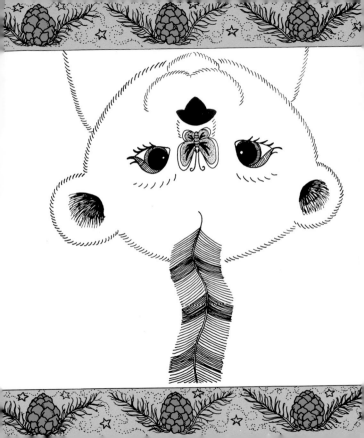

Day 20

The secret of happiness is kindness; seeing others as members of your own greater family. For every creature is your own. We are all children of one Father-Mother, God.

Day 21

The secret of happiness is doing willingly and joyfully whatever needs to be done. A flower reaches its peak of perfection when it is fully opened.

Day 22

The secret of happiness is learning from others, rather than trying to teach them. The more you show off how much you know, the more everyone will try to find flaws in your knowledge. Why are geese called "silly"? Because they honk so much!

Day 23

The secret of happiness
is not bragging, nor wanting
to be thought important. Bragging
is like a cawing crow: The louder it
caws, the more unpleasant the noise
it makes!

Day 24

The secret of happiness is love. For love is like a magical drink. The more freely you pour it out for others, the fuller and more crystal clear your own cup of happiness becomes.

Day 25

The secret of happiness is letting your smiles rise from your heart, and flow out through your eyes. People whose smiles begin only at their lips and end at their proud, uptilted noses never know the meaning of true happiness.

Day 26

The secret of happiness is doing things for others. Water that sits motionless grows stagnant. But water that flows freely remains always fresh and clear.

Day 27

The secret of happiness is strengthening people's belief in themselves. In a healthy forest, every tree stands firm.

Day 28

The secret of happiness is not avoiding difficulties. It is by climbing mountains, not by sliding down them, that a person's legs grow strong.

Happiness comes from seeing others' needs as your needs, too. It comes from seeing others' happiness as your own. A tiny cup can hold only a few drops of milk. Even so, a selfish heart can hold only a few drops of happiness. Enlarge your cup of feeling for others, and it will contain as much happiness as you can ever drink.

Day 29

Day 30

The secret of happiness is a heart reaching out in friendship to others. What would a tree be that grew no branches? Just a stick!

Day 31

The secret of happiness is concentrating on the goodness in people. For life is like a painting. To see its beauty, hold it up to the light. Even the best painting can't show its beauty if it remains hidden in a basement.

Other Books in the **Secrets** Series
by J. Donald Walters

Little Secrets of Success

Little Secrets of Friendship

Life's Little Secrets

Secrets of Love

Secrets of Happiness

Secrets of Friendship

Secrets of Inner Peace

Secrets of Success

Secrets for Men

Secrets for Women

Secrets of Prosperity

Secrets of Self-Acceptance

Secrets of Winning People

Secrets of Bringing Peace on Earth

Secrets of Leadership

Selected Other Titles
by J. Donald Walters

Education for Life - views all life as a school, and gives insights into our stages of growth and understanding.

The Path - the autobiography of J. Donald Walters.

Audio

All the World Is My Friend - children's music composed by J. Donald Walters and performed by children.

If you cannot find these titles at your local gift or bookstore, write or call: Crystal Clarity, Publishers, 14618 Tyler Foote Road, Nevada City, CA 95959, or call 1-800-424-1055.

We at Crystal Clarity, Publishers are pleased to offer you the SECRETS series, and other books, audios, and videos which embody these principles of crystal clarity:

Crystal clarity means to see oneself, and all things, as aspects of a greater reality; to seek to enter into conscious attunement with that reality; and to see all things as channels for the expression of that reality.

It means to see truth in simplicity; to seek always to be guided by the simple truth, not by opinions; and by what is, not by one's own desires or prejudices.

It means striving to see things in relation to their broadest potential.

In one's association with other people, it means seeking always to include their realities in one's own.

With clarity and common sense, these products will help you rediscover the essence of true success and lasting fulfillment in many aspects of life, such as education, leadership, business, health, relationships, and marriage. The thoughts expressed are based on timeless truths, and yet they contain the vibrancy of life on the threshold of the 21st century. If you would like a complimentary catalog, or are interested in workshops and retreats on these topics, call or write to us: Crystal Clarity, Publishers, 14618 Tyler Foote Road, Nevada City, CA 95959. 1-800-424-1055.